CHERISHED GEMSTONES FROM HISTORY

_____1606 --1831_____

Preserved Spiritual Treasure

Collected by

E. Basil Jackson

MD, JD, DLitt

TM

Post Gutenberg

AN IMPRINT OF
GLOBALEDADVANCEPRESS

CHERISHED GEMSTONES FROM HISTORY

Copyright © 2012 by E. Basil Jackson

Library of Congress Control Number: 2012951327

Jackson, E. Basil 1932 —

Cherished Gemstones from History

     (1606—1831)

--Preserved Spiritual Treasure

ISBN 978-1-935434-14-6

Subject Codes and Description: 1: REL012000: Religion: Christian Life - General 2: REL012040: Religion: Christian Life - Inspirational 3: REL012120: Religion: Christian Life – Social Issues.

Cover design by Global Graphics

Printed in Australia, Brazil, France, Germany, Italy, Spain, UK, and USA

The Press does not have ownership of the contents of a book; this is the author's work and the author owns the copyright. All theory, concepts, constructs, and perspectives are those of the author and not necessarily the Press. They are presented for open and free discussion of the issues involved. All comments and feedback should be directed to the Email: [comments4author@aol.com] and the comments will be forwarded to the author for response.

Order books from www.gea-books.com/bookstore/ or BOLDBOG@aol.com.

Published by Post-Gutenberg Books

An Imprint of
GlobalEdAdvancePRESS

DEDICATION

This work is dedicated, with deep affection to

Leila

My wife and partner
In life and in my profession.

Also to

William Moles

An Irish linguistic genius and master of
classical languages and
a dozen modern languages.
He was my instructor for both
Latin and French and is
remembered with great fondness.

Old English Chained Books

CONTENTS

.

PROLOG

Jackson -- A True Renaissance Man

E. Basil Jackson, a learned scholar of Irish roots, has gleaned the pages of sacred history and selected noteworthy words from esteemed and respected leaders of the Christian faith. These spoken and written jewels from the historical record still speak to the faith-based leaders of today.

Dr. Jackson, a reader of history and medical practitioner, is a respected academic with multiple doctorates from major universities. As such, he has made significant impact in the field of integration of religion and society. A well-traveled man skilled in several languages, Jackson has ministered to both the physical and spiritual needs of needy people around the globe. This collection of memorable expressions of wisdom and truth from the lips and pen of nearly 200 men of faith provides insight into their thinking and work as spiritual leaders.

The preservation of the archaic rendering of their words may seem out-of-date, but it retains the flavor of history in their discourse. These sayings come from revered men with historic statue who made significant contributions to the spiritual welfare of those they served. These cherished gemstones from the historical record of Christianity are words of counsel and encouragement to present leaders in faith-based groups. The quotations come from records ranging from 1606 to 1831. Some have a proverbial character while others are instructive and provide exceptional insight into the religious interaction of a noteworthy past.

– Hollis L. Green, ThD, PhD, Distinguished Professor of Education and Social Change

A Few of the Notables Quoted*

Augustine
(354 - 386) Bishop of Hippo

Lewis Bagot
(1783 -1790) Bishop of Norwich

Richard Baxter
(1615 -1691) spiritual example to John Wesley

George Wilson Bridges
(1788–1863) writer, photographer and cleric

John Calvin
(1509 –1564) influential French theologian and
leader in the Protestant Reformation

James Campbell
(1705 -1780) Scottish Presbyterian
John Chrysostom
Archbishop of Constantinople

Jonathan Edwards
(1703 -1758) American preacher/ theologian

Nicholas Felton
(1556 -1626) Bishop of Bristol

John William Fletcher
(1729 -1785) Contemporary of John Wesley

Blaise Gisbert
(1657–1731) French Jesuit rhetorician and critic

Robert Hall
(1664 -1831) English Baptist Minister

William Herbert
(1778 -1848) Dean of Manchester

Thomas Hooker
(1586 -1647) Leader in the Puritan movement

London Lives
(1690-1800) is a project dealing with
crime, poverty, and social policy.

David Livingstone
(1813 –1873) Scottish Congregationalist Medical
Missionary and explorer in Africa.

John Newton
(1725 –1807) moved from disgrace to Amazing Grace.

William Perkins
(1558 –1602) Clergy and Cambridge theologian

Robert Leightgon
(1611 - 1684) Archbishop of Glasgow

Sir Joshua Reynolds
(1723 –1792) Influential English painter

Thomas Secker
(1693 - 1768) Archbishop of Canterbury

John Wesley
(1703 –1791) Anglican cleric and theologian

---

* See a brief bio of these in the Appendix.

The teacher shows learning that shows Christ, and can be a means to distil God's graces into souls.

– W. Perkins, 1606

1606 – 1831

Do I exercise as much thought, labor, and zeal, in visiting and conversing with my people, "rebuking, exhorting, and encouraging," as I do in the preparation of my discourses for the pulpit?

– Bap. Mis. 1831

AUTHOR'S PREFACE

Some years ago, I was fortunate to buy the libraries of two Irish bishops who had passed on to their reward. What a treasure trove I discover as I spent most of my free time reviewing the collections. A discovery within the pages of a dusty theological volume was a thin paperback printed some hundreds of years before. Therein was contained some of the useful, beautiful and profound sayings now preserved in this volume.

My interest as a collector of scripted wisdom was again stimulated. This book, as well as the *Wit and Wisdom* series, is the product of that continued interest and passion. I am grateful that these nuggets of Godly wisdom will again be available to all who value the spiritual dimension and that some modern faith-based leader will be encouraged to emulate spiritually and linguistically the eminent divines of several hundred years ago. I am convinced that remembering these ancient words will benefit students, faith-based leaders, pastors, and those who occupy the pews and that their recall will glorify Christ.

All of my life I have been fascinated with and a collector of the wise sayings of those I considered to be clever, intelligent and well educated. From kindergarten on, I always, in appropriate circumstances, tried to be close to and listen to the words of those adults whom I believed I had reason to admire. This is a personality characteristic that became a lifelong practice. Even in late adulthood, I remained in close contact with my grade school teachers, high school teachers and my instructors from the days of my medical education. Some may have considered me somewhat neurotic in this regard. Every year on my visit to Ireland, the land of my birth, my greatest pleasure was my rounds to visit former teachers– at least those who were still in the land of the living.

A few years ago my high school principal died. He was probably the most intelligent person who ever honored me with friendship. William Moles was a linguistic genius. He was a master of classical languages as well as at least a dozen modern languages. He was my instructor for both Latin and French and it has been my identification and admiration for him that turned me into a language hound, although I lacked his amazing abilities. At the time of his death, he was hospitalized and knew his passing was imminent, but he was found with an open New Testament in Hungarian upon his chest.

Growing up in a Bible believing home it is not surprising that a major dimension of my identity involved preachers and Bible teachers. As a grade school boy, I remember sitting and enjoying the fantasies of having all the knowledge my teacher or the preacher seemed to possess at his fingertips.

Following training in medicine, psychiatry, addictionology, psychoanalysis, theology (with a summa cum laude in Biblical languages) and law, I eventually became the proud owner of a large library, complete with my own librarian. This had been a cumulative enterprise throughout my life. In the first grade, I gained the highest grade and received a book as a reward. This book still has a place of honor in my personal library.

My long and avid interest in the "divines" of the Christian faith was partly based on my admiration for their stand for Biblical theology without compromise. However, I was also fascinated with their beautiful and impressive use of the English language. Such skill and proficiency in grammar and syntax appears to be a lost art even for those who seek to articulate the sacred message of the Inspired Book.

- Basil Jackson

John wrote his own epitaph: "John Newton, Clerk, once an infidel and libertine, a servant of slaves in Africa, was by the rich mercy of our Lord and Saviour, Jesus Christ, preserved, pardoned and appointed to preach the Faith he had long laboured to destroy". – Newton

⊱⊰

Take heed to yourselves, lest your example contradict your doctrine ... lest you unsay with your lives, what you say with your tongues; and be the greatest hinderers of the success of your own labours. – Baxter

⊱⊰

The grand scope of the Christian ministry is to bring men home to Christ. – R. Hall

⊱⊰

Help me, thou Friend of sinners, to be nothing, to say nothing, that thou may say and do everything, and be my all in all. – Whitfield

⊱⊰

We want nothing but the return of apostolic simplicity, self-denial, and love, to bring a Pentecostal effusion of the Spirit upon our ministrations. – Bridges

Hooker used to say, "That the life of a pious clergyman was visible rhetoric;" and Herbert, that "the virtuous life of a clergyman is the most powerful eloquence." – Lives

ৡৡৡ

Our preaching ought to be above the rate of moral philosophers. Our divine orator should fetch not only his speculations and notions, but his materials for practice, from the evangelical writings: this he must do, or else he is no minister of the New Testament. – J. Edwards

ৡৡৡ

Steep your sermons in your hearts before you preach them. – Bp. Felton

ৡৡৡ

Choose rather to touch than to charm, to convert than to be admired, to force tears than applause. Give up everything to secure the salvation of your hearers. – Gisbert

ৡৡৡ

You must rather leave the ark to shake as it shall please God, than put unworthy hands to hold it up. – Lord Bacon

Our work is to open the oracles of God, even those sacred profound things that angels search into; and if God did not help us, we might soon sink under the weight of such a burden. – T. Watson

࿓࿔

Antoninus, Archbishop of Florence in the fifteenth century, is regarded as one of the founders of modern moral theology and Christian social ethics, after a long laborious life, often, in his dying moments, declared, as he had frequently done in health, "To serve God is to reign." – Church History

࿓࿔

It will not avail, to beat a man off from his drunkenness into a sober formality: a skilful master of assemblies lays his axe at the root, drives still at the heart. – Dr. Owen

࿓࿔

The great secret of ruling a church is to convince them that you love them, and say and do everything for their good. – A. Fuller

࿓࿔

Let your life be a commentary on your sermons. – Lamont

Brethren, if saving souls be your end, you will certainly intend it as well out of the pulpit as in it. – **Baxter**

❧

There is a great defect in not studying the human heart, and not taking sufficient pains to suit discourses to the actual wants of the people. – **Christian Observer, 1822**

❧

The Christian minister should endeavor to turn the eyes of every one of his hearers on himself. – **R. Hall**

❧

To give our discourses weight, it should appear that we are left to them by our texts. – **Bp. Burnet**

❧

Satan would have me while away my life in inactivity, under pretences of modesty, diffidence, and humility, and he is never wanting to furnish me with excuses for delaying or shifting services. – **T. Scott**

In my pursuits of whatever kind, let this come to my mind, "How much shall I value this on my death bed?" – President Edwards

৵৽

A sermon should be made for a text, and not a text found out for a sermon. – Burnet

৵৽

In preaching, study not to draw applauses, but groans from the hearers. – Jerome

৵৽

The good bishop is useful like the day, a general guide and comfort to us in our several paths. – Gambold

৵৽

The eloquence of a holy life is never wasted. – Christian Observer

৵৽

Our want of usefulness is often to be ascribed to our want of spirituality, much oftener than to our want of natural ability. – A. Fuller

It is greatly to be deplored that there are so many preachers who seem to aim at pleasing by studying to say what is calculated to surprise and astonish, rather than to instruct and improve. – Eclectic, 1826

෯ක

Is it no disgrace for a minister of the gospel to waste his time in idleness? – MacGill

෯ක

When we have preached, we have but sown the seed, still we must look to God to water it. – M. Henry's Sermons

෯ක

The teacher shows learning that shows Christ, and can be a means to distil God's graces into souls. – W. Perkins, 1606

෯ක

Ambition and pride are the rankest poison in the church, when they are possessed by preachers. – Luther's Table Talk

He that considers himself as the father of his flock will not forget with what mildness, tenderness, and love, a father treats his children. – Stowel's Life of Bp. Wilson

༄ৎ

When we preach rather words than matter, they catch people's ears, not their souls. – T. Watson

༄ৎ

While we listen to the din of our own praises, we shall feel a fire that consumes the heart, rather than a shower that refreshes it. – Campbell

༄ৎ

The devil, in the last day, shall rise against us in condemnation, for that he hath been more careful to get souls than we to save them. – Bernard

༄ৎ

Cold and lifeless, though never so fine and well contrived, must those discourses be, that are of an unknown Christ. – Leighton

A pastor's life should be vocal; his sermons must be practiced as well as preached.
– Dr. Owen

ঌৎ

Deeply consider that to be successful in bringing souls to God, you must bring the spirit of the gospel into the work of the ministry.
– Dr. A. Clarke

ঌৎ

Am I more fit to serve and to enjoy God than I was last week? **– S. Pearce**

ঌৎ

I see that spirituality of mind is the main qualification for the work of the ministry.
– Urquhart

ঌৎ

Sitting down among my books, I dare not reach forth my hand to any of them, till I have first looked up to Heaven, and craved favor of Him to whom all my studies are duly referred; without whom, I can neither profit nor labor.
– Bp. Hall's Life

Preach without restraint; intercede warmly; invite powerfully; persuade forcibly; urge incessantly, the great salvation: cry aloud, "Whosoever will, let him take of the water of life freely." – Gilbert's Address to Pritchard

☙❧

I observe in my mind a sinful anxiety to preach well, rather than a holy anxiety to preach usefully. – Hinton

☙❧

A sermon that has more head infused into it than heart will not come home with efficacy to the hearers. – Cecil

☙❧

Since I began to beg God's blessing on my studies, I have done more in one week than I have done in a whole year before. – Dr. Payson

☙❧

Leave Christ out of your sermons and you blot the sun out of the firmament. – R. Watson

To win a soul is your noblest prize; and the greater number you win, the brighter and richer will be that "crown of rejoicing," which you will wear in the day of the Lord.
– R. Watson

☙

Do I exercise as much thought, labor, and zeal, in visiting and conversing with my people, "rebuking, exhorting, and encouraging," as I do in the preparation of my discourses for the pulpit? **– Bap. Mis. 1831**

☙

In the first evangelic times, ministers were distinguished from other Christians, by their spiritual knowledge, and sanctity of life.
– Milton

☙

A discourse to be profitable must come home to our own case. **– Grimshawe**

☙

In most cases, those ministers who are most indefatigable in their exertions, and most fervent in their prayers, are honoured with the greatest success. **– D. Barker**

To make a sermon, and Christ not the main thing in it, you may call it discoursing, it is not preaching. – R. Hall, of Kelso

❧

Be faithfulness, rather than fame, your chief object. – Bp. Bagot

❧

Three things make a divine – meditation, prayer, and temptation; and three things are to be done by a minister:

1. To read the bible over and over;

2. To pray earnestly;

3. Always to be a learner.

– Luther

❧

In every sermon let something be practical. How often has it been found, that when ministers have felt most embarrassed, the most effectual good has been done to the people. O for hearts entirely resigned to the will of God.
– S. Pearce to Dr. Ryland

I long to think, to speak, to act as one stepping into eternity. – J. Townsend's Diary

ॐ

All men are orators when they feel. The language of the heart has an unction, and an energy, which no eloquence or sublimity can reach. A minister should not only be a director, but a leader; he should not only point out the way, but walk before his flock in it. – Bp. Hopkins

ॐ

Let thy studies be not so much upon the pleasant and ornamental parts of learning, as the useful; such as may enrich thy thoughts, inform thy judgment, regulate thy life, and fit thee for thy station. – Dr. T. Fuller

ॐ

Such eloquence as makes the hearers look grave, and, as it were, out of countenance, are the properest. – Bp. Burnet

ॐ

The life and the power of godliness in the heart, will give that affection, warmth, and pathos to the pulpit addresses, which the learning and rhetoric of the schools may chasten and direct, but cannot excite. – Congregational Mag. 1828

The eternal salvation and damnation of souls are not to be treated off with jests and witticisms. – South

❧

Nothing is greater bar to a minister's usefulness, or renders him and his labours more contemptible, than a known attachment to money, a griping fist, and a hard heart. – Preacher's Manual

❧

Stir up yourself to the work with sacred vigour, that the assembly may feel what you speak. – Dr. Watts

❧

Although God honours faithfulness in his servants, he will yet be honoured himself, first and chief. – C. Colton

❧

Nothing is gained by driving and scolding. Everything almost may be done by drawing, and melting, and winning. – D. Stoner's Life

Ordinary callings are not learned without a long apprenticeship, and will the art of governing should be learned on a sudden?
– Scougal

࿐

A minister has not done his duty to the heathen, if he has not instructed his people in their duty to them. – American Tract

࿐

It is said of the late Rev. L. Richmond, that "Christ Jesus was the soul of all his discourses;" every precept, every promise, derived its force and value from his bearing and relation to Him. – Grimshawe

࿐

The question at last will be, not how many things have you learned? But how much have you taught? – Bp. Jewel

࿐

Unless you have soul prosperity as Christians, you will not have pleasure in your work as ministers. – Massillon

What! Shall a Christian minister consume his valuable time in ease and indolence! – **Massillon**

ॐ∽ॐ

The chief end of an orator is to persuade; therefore, that preacher, who only flourishes in general notions, and does not aim at some particular argument, is like an unwise fisher, who spreads his net to the empty air, where he cannot expect any success of his labours.
– Bp. Wilkins

ॐ∽ॐ

When Pericles, the Athenian orator, went to address the people, he prayed to the gods that nothing might go out of his mouth but what might be to the purpose. A good example for preachers. – **Bradbury**

ॐ∽ॐ

The Jesuits, who study human nature diligently, discover more earnestness in their discourses than other preachers. – **D'Oyley**

ॐ∽ॐ

Let earnest prayers for the down-pouring of the Spirit on your hearers precede and follow your sermons. – **Dr. Erskine**

Nothing is so disagreeable as a discourse of a formal, starched air, which speaks, acts, walks, and moves by exact measure. – Gisbert

৵৽

If the good of souls be not before thy heart, thou canst not expect God's blessing. – Crombie

৵৽

The office of "fellow-worker with God," would have been no mean honour to have been conferred upon the archangel nearest the everlasting throne. – Bridges

৵৽

The minister purchases his happiness at a dear rate, who suffers his people to sleep in their sins. – C. Winter's Letters

৵৽

When once an idea is clearly expressed, every additional stroke will only confuse the mind and diminish the effect. – Kirke White

We should be jealous of the praise and honour which come from men, and seek only the honour and approbation of God. – A. Reed

❧

I love the ministrations of those who are the most searching. – Dr. Ryland

❧

Brethren, it is easier to declaim, like an orator, against a thousand sins in others, than to mortify one sin in ourselves; to be more industrious in our pulpits, than in our closets; to preach twenty sermons to our people, than one to our own hearts. – Flavel

❧

Our churches will forgive almost any fault in a minister, rather than dullness. – Hinton

❧

He that will do good in the ministry must be careful as the fisher to do nothing to scare souls away from him, but allure and invite, that they may be toiled within the compass of the net. – Gurnall

The pulpit should be free from both colloquial pleasantry, and repulsive gloom. – Leifchild

৵৽

I longed to be, as a flame of fire, continually glowing in the divine service, preaching and building up Christ's kingdom to my latest, to my dying hour. – Brainerd

৵৽

The more we do, the more we may do in the service of God. – P. Henry

৵৽

No character on earth so ill, accords with a proud, imperious spirit, as that of a Christian pastor. – A. Booth

৵৽

He is approved of God, and he alone who preaches what he feels; who daily lives upon the truths his fervent lips proclaim. – Gibbons

I spent time in prayer for the Divine assistance in my studies. – Boston

❧

The sacred ministry is not a state of idleness or of pleasure, but a holy warfare, in which there are always toils and fatigues to be endured. Whoever is not resolved courageously to maintain the interests of Christ, and to labour continually to enlarge his kingdom, is not fit for this warfare. – Quesnel

❧

To save one soul is worth a man's coming into the world, and richly worth the labours of his whole life. – Burnet

❧

Your work is to save souls. You are shepherds, and must know all your sheep, and what is their disease, and mark their straying, and help to cure them, and fetch them home. – Baxter

❧

Simply to be good should not content you; you should endeavour to excel. – Grove

I do not wish for any heaven upon earth besides that of preaching the precious gospel of Christ to immortal souls. May these weak desires increase and strengthen with every difficulty.
– H. Martyn

આ∞◎

It has been observed by some eminent divines, that ministers are seldom honoured with much success, unless they are continually aiming at the conversion of sinners. **– Dr. Owen**

આ∞◎

Preachers by making light of common truths, and indulging in a spirit of curious speculation, will render preaching rather an entertainment, than a benefit to the soul.
– A. Fuller

આ∞◎

Speech of man's self, ought to be seldom and well chosen. **– Lord Bacon**

આ∞◎

What have I done this day for the souls and bodies of God's dear saints? **– John Fletcher**

Let the clergy live and labour well, and they will feel, that as much authority will follow, as they will know how to manage well.
– Bp. Burnet

ক্ক

Seriousness in a minister is agreeable, not only to the serious, but to men of all tempers.
– Paley

ক্ক

For a person to leave public worship in raptures with the minister's abilities is no proof that he has received spiritual benefit.
– A. Booth

ক্ক

A sick conscience spoils the tongue of the eloquent, and makes it stammer. **– Ambrose**

ক্ক

You must restrain your copiousness, lest you expand it into feebleness; you must often severely chastise the inventive faculties, lest, whilst you occupy the imagination, you miss the conscience. **– R. Watson**

O that the ministry of Scotland may be kept from destroying the Church of Scotland.
– **Halyburton**

෫ඁ෴

Never make an unprofitable visit. When the celebrated Thomas Hooker had heard the Rev. Jonathan Burr, the puritan, preach, he observed, "Surely this man will not long be out of heaven: he preaches as if he were there already." – **Brook's Puritans**

෫ඁ෴

Ministers will never do much good till they begin to pull sinners out of the fire.
– **Sutcliff, of Olney**

෫ඁ෴

Human eloquence should be subservient to the word of God, and not the word of God made the slave of human eloquence. – **Austin**

෫ඁ෴

What man on earth is so pernicious a drone as an idle minister? – **Cecil**

What is more odious than a finical, conceited, dressed-up young minister, who thinks he is the mighty orator? – Mr. Thornton's Letter to C. Winter

⁂

Be servant-like, but not servile. – Whitfield to Winter

⁂

Figures are the ornaments of speech, and ornaments lose their effect by being set too thick. – Preacher's Manual

⁂

How difficult! how dreadful! To preach an unknown Saviour! – Bridges

⁂

If it pleases the Lord to let his faithful ministers suffer, it is either because their testimony is finished, or because He will receive more honour by their suffering. – Hildersham

How shall he communicate knowledge with his lips, who hath not a treasure of it in his mind?
– Gelling

❧

The husbandman doth not more constantly go forth with his spade, to perform his daily labour in the field, than the minister is to go and dig in the mine of scripture. **– Gurnall**

❧

Let your constant aim be to humble the sinner, to exalt the Saviour, and to promote holiness.
– C. Mather

❧

Have blank books, in which note with your pen, the notable things which you meet with in reading. **– C. Mather**

❧

Let usefulness, usefulness to the souls of men, be your grand and perpetual aim.
– Dr. H.F. Burder

Christian pastors should retain the character, and cherish the spirit and habits of a student, when the name is laid aside. – Massillon

അ⊸ഔ

The spirit of our ministry is a spirit of separation from the world; of prayer, of labour, of zeal, of knowledge, of piety. – Massillon

അ⊸ഔ

Knowledge, you must remember, is the fruit of patient observation and study, not of spontaneous growth. – Leifchild

അ⊸ഔ

Keep not your religion for the pulpit: have it at heart and at hand, at dinner and at tea, and let every occurrence furnish you with a subject for spiritual improvement. – Cor. Winter

അ⊸ഔ

There is nothing out of heaven, next to Christ, dearer to me than my ministry. – Rutherford

A dry sermon can never be a good one. – Blair

❧

The puritans visited their flocks by house-row; the visits were short: they talked a little for God, and then concluded with prayer to God. – Berridge

❧

A good style is constituted by proper words in proper places. – W. Jones

❧

The words of a preacher should be those of a guilty man to guilty men; of a dying man to dying men; of a man who humbly hopes he has found pardon for himself, and is most affectionately anxious that his hearers may find the same blessing. – Dwight

❧

Let us speak to our people as for their lives. – Baxter

Are not those ministers usually the most happy and the most successful, who display the kindest solicitude for the juvenile division of their flock? – Dr. H.F. Burder

చ≈≪

Never be anywhere, nor in any temper, that would unfit you for preaching. – S. Bradburn

చ≈≪

Mere moral preaching tells the people how the house ought to be built; gospel preaching actually builds the house. – Toplady

చ≈≪

I find I cannot study to advantage without a plan. – Urquhart

చ≈≪

What has become of all those hours, which we professed to spend in prayer before God, with the bible in our hands, and our ministry in our hearts? – Bp. D. Wilson

My days roll away with but little done for God; and this is my burden. – Brainerd

࿇

I hope I have had; and shall, if I live, still have many sermons sent down from heaven. – J. Hinton

࿇

Think not how can I make a sermon soonest and easiest, but how can I make the most profitable sermon for my hearers. – Dr. Watts

࿇

The devil does not care how ministers are employed, if it is not in their proper work. – Cecil

࿇

That is not the best sermon which makes the hearers go away talking to one another, and praising the speaker, but which makes them go away thoughtful, and serious, and hastening to be alone. – Bp. Burnet

Guard against a love of pleasure, a sensual temper, and indulgence of appetite, and excessive relish of wine and dainties; this carnalizes the soul, and gives occasion to the world to reproach but too justly. – Dr. Watts

∂∞∂

The assuming magisterial airs in the pulpit is contemptible. – J. Cooke

∂∞∂

Robert Bolton, B.D., who died 1631, entered so deeply into the work of the ministry, that he said, "He never delivered a sermon to his people in public, till he had preached it to himself in private. – Ambrose

∂∞∂

Frequently visit your Sunday schools, if it is only to walk through them. – Baxter

∂∞∂

I have these forty years been sensible of the sin of losing time: I could not spare an hour. – Baxter

In no one sermon I ever preached, had I one lesson for myself and another for my hearers; my heart and conscience always made part of my audience. – Skelton

᠁

If I want a man to fly, I must contrive to find him wings: if I would successfully enforce moral duties, I must advance evangelical motives. – J. Newton

᠁

Never did any minister repent of his labor in catechizing. – Dr. C. Mather

᠁

East and west, north and south, are all indifferent to me, provided I have an opportunity of advancing the glory of our Lord. – Xavier

᠁

To preach the gospel properly, is to handle every subject of discourse, so as to keep Christ continually in the view of the hearers. – Dr. Owen

Be calm in general, in order to be vehement when the proper juncture shall arrive. – **Reybaz**

కా

Discourses containing little that awakens drowsy attention, little that enforces plainly and home what men must do to be saved, leave them as unreformed as ever, and only lull them in a fatal security. – **Abp. Secker**

కా

A minister's acceptance and usefulness depends as much on his conduct as Religion Explained: The Human Instincts That Fashion Gods, Spirits and Ancestors, Basic Books, 2001 on his talents. – **Massillon**

కా

My brethren, a pastor who does not pray, who does not love prayer, does not belong to that church which prays without ceasing. – **Massillon**

కా

True eloquence is the art of placing truth in the most advantageous light for conviction and persuasion. – **Blair**

To be excessively heated, when the subject admits only of moderate warmth, is a kind of madness out of season. – Gisbert

☙❧

Discouragements, properly sustained and carefully improved, will become the most fruitful sources of eventual encouragement in the Christian ministry, and love to our work bears us on in the midst of, and above all our difficulties. – Bridges

☙❧

Be concerned much more to persuade than to please. – Blair

☙❧

Wicked ministers are like those statues, which in old time were set up in cross ways, with their arms extended to point out the road to passengers, but themselves walked not in them. – Bp. Hopkins

☙❧

Let us aim in every sermon to please God, and profit our people; to do them good, rather than gain applause. – Mason

When nations are to perish in their sins, 'Tis in the church the leprosy begins. – Cowper

అ∽ఆ

My witness both within and above me knows, and my pained breast upon the Lord's day at night, that my desire to have Christ awful, and amiable, and sweet, to my people, is now my joy; and it was my desire and aim to make Christ and them one. – Rutherford, in prison, 1637

అ∽ఆ

They, who are sent to preach, will preach as others cannot, because they preach what they know and enjoy. – E. Parsons

అ∽ఆ

I hope you are diligent in that most useful work of catechizing. – Abp. Secker

అ∽ఆ

The Christian minister should not dare to amuse his hearers by sporting witticisms, or exhibiting eccentricities. – Eclectic, 1816

It was said of Eliot, the distinguished missionary, by many of his friends, "I was never with him, but I got, or might have got, good from him." – Lives

≈∞≈

A minister who is full of love to Christ and souls cannot be a loiterer. – N. Vincent

≈∞≈

He, who does not prepare what to say to the people, tempts God to come out of his ordinary way to his assistance; and he who depends entirely upon his own preparations, makes a god of his gifts. – Nesbit

≈∞≈

Those only ought to be chosen into the priesthood whom God will hear. – Cyprian

≈∞≈

We are accountable for the spirit of our congregations, since a minister, who is beloved by his people, can cause the tone of their character to strike in unison with his own. – J. A. James

Ministers cannot be too often told that they should leave the world to the people of the world. – **Quesnel**

❧

Let every text have its true meaning, every truth its due weight, every hearer his proper portion. – **D. Barker**

❧

I am convinced we shall never be eminently useful, till both ourselves and our flocks do more honor to the Divine Spirit, and live more fully under his light and power. – **D. Barker**

❧

A minister who is "a man pleaser," is a soul destroyer. – **Cooke**

❧

Dr. Johnson observes of Dr. Watts, that "Whatever he took in hand was, by his incessant solicitude for souls, converted into theology." – **Life of Watts**

A lover of his appetites, and a slave to his taste, makes but a mean figure among men, and a very scurvy one among clergymen.
– Bp. Burnet

౼∽

We separate too much our ministerial from our pastoral office. **– J. W. Cunningham**

౼∽

The destruction of the eastern churches commenced in the falling away of their pastors.
– J. W. De La Flechere

౼∽

The way of preaching should correspond with its design, which is to inform the mind and move the heart. **– Gelling**

౼∽

As your studies, so your prayers are to be directed to your work as a minister.
– Job Orton

Shall we spare labor, when Christ spared not his own blood? – **Abp. Leighton**

࿊

A minister ought to be adorned with all the virtues, and to give an example to others. His conversation should not be according to the ordinary way of men, but like to the angels in heaven. – **Kempis**

࿊

Every discourse that wants an interpreter is a very bad one. – **Rollin**

࿊

O sirs, how many have preached Christ, and perished for want of a saving interest in him! – **Baxter**

࿊

The merchant, if he mistakes in his venture, wastes an estate; the statesman, if he fail in his duty, ruins a kingdom; the minister, if he fails in his, damns the soul! – **A. Reed**

Some eloquent preachers are like those fine artists who paint windows, and thereby obscure, and in too many instances exclude the light. – Lamont

❧❧

The action of the theatre, and the bombast of romances, are unworthy of the pulpit, and disgrace its solemnity.　– Lamont

❧❧

The desire of the conversion of souls is nothing else but spiritualized humanity. – Howe

❧❧

It is remarkable, that the charges exhibited by our Lord against the seven churches of Asia, are all addressed to the respective ministers of those churches. – Dr. Fawcett

❧❧

The most splendid talents, and the most mighty eloquence, and the most devoted diligence, will be utterly inefficient, except the unction be brought down from heaven by frequent and fervent supplication. – Bridges

What shall I say, and how shall I say it, so as to glorify God, and benefit the souls of men?
– Bostwick

৵৵

Let it be a maxim with you never to preach without introducing Christ and the Holy Spirit.
– Doddridge

৵৵

I will be ready to do offices of kindness and love, not for the praise of men, or to purchase commendation, but out of conscience to the command of God. **– Richard Mather**

৵৵

The late Rev. Henry Martyn was known at the university by the designation of "The man who never wasted an hour." **– Dr. Campbell**

৵৵

We may say justly, that in ninety-nine cases out of a hundred, if a pastor is despised, he has himself to blame. **– Dr. Campbell**

He, who affects a show of learning throughout his discourses, will convince the undiscerning that he is learned, and the better judges that he is ridiculous. – Gisbert

৵৽

Faith is the master-spring of a preacher. – Cecil

৵৽

I consider that man as having attained the end of preaching, who constrains his hearer to forget everything else except the way in which he is personally affected by the great and interesting truths brought before him. – Innes

৵৽

I hear with pleasure the voice of that preacher, whose endeavor is to excite in me saving compunction, and not to attract vain applause. – Bernard

৵৽

I would rather be a condemned minister of God, than the greatest prince on earth. – Halyburton

The conversion of one soul is of inconceivably more value than the temporal salvation of a world. – Lavater

❧

Every day shall be distinguished by at least one particular act of love. – Lavater

❧

When we go to study, let us pray to God to put a word into our mouth that may suit the case, and reach the consciences of those to whom we are to speak. – M. Henry

❧

It may be that my parish forgets me; but my witness is in heaven, I do not forget them: they are my sighs in the night and my tears in the day.
– Rutherford

❧

An orator without sensibility cannot attain the highest end of his labors – affect the heart, while he informs the understanding.
– Reybaz

A minister who does not habituate himself to devout prayer, may deliver animated discourses, and substitute address and elocution for zeal and piety; but you will always see the man; you will perceive, that it is not the fire which descends from heaven.
– Massillon

⊱⊰

Fear nothing so much as self-confidence.
– Dr. Rippon

⊱⊰

Such preachers as think themselves too wise to learn, will, sooner or later, be thought by others too weak to teach. **– Dr. Rippon**

⊱⊰

When you pen your sermons, little do you think that you are drawing up indictments against your own soul? **– Baxter**

⊱⊰

It is said that Whitfield preached as one who had the future world, with all its dread solemnities, immediately in his eye.
– Dr. C. Mather

My journeys must, like my visits, be for nothing but that God may be served in them.
– Dr. C. Mather

❧

Let us remember what pains our Lord and Master took with one single, sinful woman, at Jacob's well. – **Benson**

❧

I have been cured of expecting the Holy Spirit's influence without due preparation on our part, by observing how men preach who take up that error. I have heard such men talk nonsense by the hour. – Cecil

❧

I wonder we are not more energetic, and active, and faithful, when roused on the one hand by the love of Christ, and on the other by the dangerous situation of our fellow sinners.
– D. Barker

❧

In studying a sermon, be more concerned about what the people stand in need of, than about gaining their applause, for having preached a fine, useless sermon. – **Bradburn**

False prophets care only to please. – Bp. Hall

❧

When Chrysostom was ordained to the ministry, he had such notions of the duty incumbent upon him, that he told his friends, he thought his soul would have been torn from his body. – Sozomen

❧

It is almost as easy to keep fish alive without water, as to preserve spirituality of mind amid the smiles of the world. – Chrysostom

❧

A minister had need look to it that he profit by all his preaching himself. – J. Rogers

❧

Do you value yourself upon popular applause and a great name? Think how many who have made a distinguished figure in the world, are dead and unregarded, as if they had never been. – Seed

A sermon to be good must be good tempered.
– Edw. Parsons

৯~৯

In many cases a copious manner of expression gives strength and weight to our ideas, which oft make impressions upon the mind, as iron does upon solid bodies, rather by repeated strokes than a single blow. **– Pliny's letters**

৯~৯

Your own family should be a picture of what you wish other families to be. **– Cecil**

৯~৯

When the care of souls is the matter of trust, let the greater part of men standoff, and presume not to meddle in the mighty work.
– Chrysostom

৯~৯

The success of the ministry will always depend, humanly speaking, upon the fervor with which the divinity of Christ is presented to the mind of man. **– J. Parsons**

Preachers in their sermons should resemble heralds, declaring the message of their Master.
– Quesnel

᚛ॐ᚛

A man sometimes suffers himself to be lulled asleep by the agreeable voice of a flattering world, which praises the pastor for performing one half of his duty, while God condemns him for the neglect of the other. **– Quesnel**

᚛ॐ᚛

Let us not refuse disgrace; Jesus Christ was disgraced for us: may our disgrace tend to his glory. **– Life of Fenelon**

᚛ॐ᚛

It is a sad thing, when a sermon shall have that one thing, the Spirit of God, wanting in it.
– Life of Eliot

᚛ॐ᚛

We cannot but doubt the genuine tone of healthful spirituality, without an industrious habit. **– Bridges**

If anything but usefulness will satisfy us, I do not wonder that we are not useful. – T. Scott

❧

The Lord is to make use of me as he pleaseth. – **Boston**

❧

The man who can pass days in listening to folly and profanity, in the company of the rich, cannot stoop to converse with the poor on the concerns of the soul, and the difficulties of their lowly state. – **Dr. MacGill**

❧

Too close a thread of reason, too great an abstraction of thought, too sublime and too metaphysical a strain, are suitable to very few auditories, if to any at all. – Burnet

❧

A cold delivery of common place matter does not touch the heart. – **Christian Observe**

A minister who lives an idle life may preach with truth and reason, or as did the Pharisees; but not as Christ, or as one having authority.
– Bp. Taylor

৵৹৻

Some think they cannot be faithful, unless they are furious: whatever mercy may be in their message, there is none in their delivery.
– J. Thornton

৵৹৻

It has been observed of Luther, by Melanchthon, that "Whatever he said went to the heart, and in a wondrous manner penetrated the minds of men." – Quesnel

৵৹৻

A minister ought not to wander from house to house from human motives. – Quesnel

৵৹৻

Should success accompany your labors, there will be the greatest necessity to guard against pride and self-esteem. – A. Booth

There is a peculiar majesty in unaffected plainness; a substantial beauty, which needs neither patch nor paint. – Lamont

ॐ

How often does pride choose our subject, and more often choose our words and ornaments. – Baxter

ॐ

He who has a happy talent for parlor preaching, has sometimes done more for Christ and souls in a few minutes, than by the labor of many days in the usual course of public preaching. – Watts

ॐ

Let us consider how little has been our success in comparison of the multitudes converted by our fathers in the ministry! – Jennings

ॐ

To use the same manner and matter in all auditories is as if a person should make all wearable goods of an equal size, for children and men, large and small. – Bp. Wilkins

There is something in an affectionate statement of gospel truths, peculiarly calculated to find its way to the heart.
– Jerram

⤷⤶

If you have great talents, industry will improve them; if you have but moderate abilities, industry will supply their deficiencies.
– Sir Joshua Reynolds

⤷⤶

The least degree of ambiguity, which leaves the mind in suspense as to the meaning, ought to be avoided with the greatest care. – Blair

⤷⤶

One of the chief parts of the pastoral care is the visiting of the sick. – Burnet

⤷⤶

For want of a spirit for study there are many saunterers, and have been many scandals among ministers. – A. Fuller

How can we be converted by apostles we cannot understand? – De La Bruyere

కావ

True teachers must first have the Son of righteousness to shine in their own hearts, before they can enlighten with his light.
– W. Perkins

కావ

We esteem the most plain and simple preachers, provided they be sensible and correct, the most eloquent.
– Preacher's Manual

కావ

Those who know most should still continue to learn. – Gelling

కావ

Pulpit discourses should resemble a clear mirror; they should give the hearers a faithful representation of themselves. – T. Watson

God will bless your endeavors, not your idleness. – Bridges

❧

Every minister should engage both his head and his heart in his work: his head with labor, and his heart with love. – T. Watson

❧

He, who solicitously seeks to distinguish himself in the pulpit by a display of elegance and profundity of learning, proves himself deficient in some of the leading virtues which ought to characterize a Christian minister. – Gisborne

❧

We lose more than we gain in the minds of our hearers, when we would conciliate their esteem by the sacrifice of our duty. – Massillon

❧

Have you permitted greediness of studies to eat up other duties? – Dr. Owen

Surely, that preaching which comes from the soul, most works on the soul. – Dr. T. Fuller

ঌঌ

It is said of the Rev. Joseph Alleine, that when he came to any house to take up his abode there, he brought salvation with him; when he departed, he left salvation behind him. – Lives

ঌঌ

If a man has a dry, logical, scholastic turn of mind, we shall rarely find him an interesting preacher. – Cecil

ঌঌ

Did we know and enjoy Christ more, how active would it make us in his service; how zealous for his glory; how impatient of the disgrace, which men, full of themselves, but empty of Christ, are casting upon him! – Hurrion

ঌঌ

My brethren, dull and pointless arrows are ill suited to pierce the conscience of hardened sinners. – Dr. Erskine

The art of fine speaking is one thing, that of persuasion another. – Howe

જ્જ

When we see how little is done, how little effect the gospel has, for the most part, it may make many a sad misgiving heart among us. – Howe

જ્જ

Exclaim and thunder against vice, but spare and respect persons. – Gisbert

જ્જ

Luther has observed, that he always found himself in the best temper for study, when he had first composed his thoughts, and raised up his affections by prayer. – Luther

જ્જ

I fear many things, which employ a large portion of our retired time, are studied rather as polite amusements to our own minds, than as things which seem to have any apparent subservience to the glory of God, and the edification of our flock. – Doddridge

Is the skill and discernment employed in increasing the resources and glory of earthly kingdoms, to be compared with the divine science of saving immortal souls?
– Grimshawe's Life of Richmond

❧

Under the law even the daughters of the priests were, for the same sins with others, condemned to greater punishment, on account of the pre-eminence of their fathers. – Deut. Ix. 22

❧

Oh! How much easier is it to preach from the understanding than from the heart! – Bridges

❧

Have a care that you lose not what you have to say, while you are wholly taken up with considering how to say it artfully. – Austin

❧

Take heed to yourselves, my dearest brethren. Many ministers, who opened the way to heaven to others, are now in hell for want of humility.
– Xavier

The heart of Dr. W. Gouge was so much in his work that he often said to Lord Coventry, then keeper of the great seal, that he envied not his situation. – Lives

❧

Obscurity in the discourse is an argument of ignorance in the mind. – Bp. Wilkins

❧

The chief characteristics of the eloquence suited to the pulpit, as distinguished from the other kinds of public speaking, appear to be these two – gravity and warmth. – Blair

❧

An eager desire to say what is curious and uncommon, is a dangerous turn of mind in a teacher of Christianity. – Dr. Erskine

❧

There has seldom been an instance of a declension of a minister which has not been preceded by too much of social festivity.
– J. Campbell

I prayed that the Lord would be with me: for the pulpit without him was a terror. – **Boston**

❧

Too great a portion of time may be spent in even innocent society. – **Dr. MacGill**

❧

Ministers are under strong temptations, when called to preach on special occasions, to consult human authorities instead of the word of God. – **J. Cooke**

❧

When pastors envy each other's gifts, success, and estimation, the poor church suffers. – **N. Vincent**

❧

The divine, who spends all his time in study and contemplation, on objects ever so sublime and glorious, while his people are left uninstructed, acts the same part the eagle would do, that should sit all day staring at the sun, while her young ones were starving in the nest. – **Horne**

Sermons ought to be very plain. The figures must be easy; not mean, but noble, and brought into the design to make it better understood.
— Burnet

‍

A minister, by preaching twenty years with the tongue of an angel, shall not edify his hearers so much, as he shall corrupt his seers by one material slip in his conduct. — Skelton

‍

To speak coldly and slightly of heavenly things, is nearly as bad as to say nothing of them.
— Baxter

‍

To ascertain the true meaning of the words and phrases used by those who "spake as they were moved by the Holy Ghost," ought to be the single aim of the theologian.
— Hist. Of Enthusiasm

‍

Your piety must be undoubted, and manifest to all. — Leifchild

He, who thinks to furnish himself out of plays and romances with language for the pulpit, shows himself much fitter to act a part in the revels, than for a cure of souls. – South

☙❧

The readiest way of finding access to a man's heart, is to go into his house. – Dr. Chalmers

☙❧

Follow not the practice of those who seek wisdom only in learning. – Osborn

☙❧

The man that issues from frequent and long retirement will ascend the pulpit as Aaron entered the tabernacle of the congregation, when the holy oil had been poured upon his head, and the fragrance filled the place. – Jay

☙❧

It was a high eulogy pronounced upon T. Gataker, B.D., as a minister, when it was said, that he was more ambitious of doing good to others than of exalting himself. – Brook

O that I could spend all my time for God!
– Brainerd

৵৽৹

Of the Rev. Edmund Trench, who died in 1689, it is observed, "His time was truly divided betwixt beholding the face of his Father in heaven, and ministering to the heirs of salvation on earth. **– Lives**

৵৽৹

Fit words are better than fine; for fit words are always fine, but fine words are not always fit.
– Venning

৵৽৹

Avoid such stories, whose mention may suggest bad thoughts to the auditors, and use not a light comparison to make thereof a grave application, for fear lest the poison go further than the antidote. **– Dr. T. Fuller**

৵৽৹

In your visits to the houses of your flock, depart not without putting in some word for God and religion. **– Dr. Watts**

Ministers should go up into the pulpit to preach the word of God in his name, with that strength of faith, as to be assured that their doctrine can no more be overthrown than God himself.
– Calvin, Com. on 2 Cor. Iii

৵৽

Blessed be God, I feel myself to be his minister.
– Henry Martyn

৵৽

My attention to the classics has made me very squeamish in my Christian studies.
– Dr. Middleton

৵৽

A sermon, like a tool, may be polished till it has no edge. – Orton

৵৽

Of what avail is our knowledge, if it be not sanctified to the work of God!
– Bridges

Does not a careful shepherd look after every individual sheep? A good physician attends every particular patient? Should not the shepherd and physician of the church take heed to every individual member of his charge?
– Baxter

Urge what you say, as a man would plead for his own life, and as if it were your last sermon.
– Bradburn

Can you make the arrow wound where it will not stick? Have any of your soft harangues, your continued threads of silken eloquence, ever raised the dead? – Watts

Be familiar with your people; not high, or strange. Converse with them for their good.
– M. Henry

You can never truly teach humility, or tell what it is, unless you practice it yourselves.
– Bp. Taylor

*I know of no scriptural way of preaching
to men, otherwise than as sinners.*
– L. Richmond

৵৽

*Leighton, when asked whether he preached
to the times, as was usual in the seventeenth
century, made this reply: "If all the brethren
have preached to the times, may not one poor
brother be suffered to preach on eternity?*
– John Wesley

৵৽

*What sermons are attended with the greatest
blessing? Such as are most close, convincing,
and searching – such as have in them most
of Christ – such as urge the heinousness of
men's living in contempt or ignorance of Him.*
– John Wesley

৵৽

*Never have what may be called favorite
expressions.* **– Gisbert**

৵৽

*Tell the sinner the worst of himself, to drive
him from himself to the suitable, appointed,
surprising, and profound relief – redemption
through the blood of Christ.* **– J. Cooke**

The worst encomium that can be given to a Christian discourse is to say, it is witty.
– Gisbert

⮞⮜

After so long a suspension from serving the Redeemer in his church, my soul pants for usefulness more extensive than ever, and I long to become an apostle to the world. – S. Pearce

⮞⮜

It is observed of the late Dr. A. Thompson, that his presence was enough to repress anything which had the semblance of irreligion.
– A. Thompson

⮞⮜

I exhort you, my dear youth, on no consideration to take up preaching merely as a science. – Winter to Jay

⮞⮜

The celebrated Rev. T. Harmer had a pair of salt-cellars, on which were engraved in Greek capitals the words ΥΜΕΙΣ ΕΣΤΕ ΤΟ ΑΛΑΣ ΤΗΣ ΤΗΣ,
(ye are the salt of the earth.)
A useful memento to all ministers.

Of all men living, the preacher of the gospel has the most need of energy: he preaches for eternity.

૰ৡৡ

"Were the Lord to make me young again," said the pious and zealous Mr. Brown on his deathbed, *"I should study to devise some other means for the gaining of souls, than those which I have used, and prosecute them with more activity than I ever did."* – **Lives**

૰ৡৡ

He is untrue to the spirit and obligations of his office, who would not for the sake of souls willingly hazard all the rewards and honors of literary estimation. – **Chalmers**

૰ৡৡ

I find that ministry most efficient, and indeed that ministry alone efficient, in which the doctrine of the cross of Christ obtains the same prominence with which it was exhibited in the preaching of the apostles themselves. – **Dr. Burder**

It is a small thing to inform the understanding with doctrine, except also the heart be reformed by exhortation. – Paul Baynes

৵৽

Saturday evening was his regular season for special devotion, for a due preparation for the Sabbath. – J. Hinton's Life

৵৽

Frequently ask yourselves, while composing your discourses is this likely to be of any service in converting men? – Anthony Burgess

৵৽

To preach God's word as it is our opinion, our interest, our advantage, is sinful; yet how apt are we to regard a truth as it is ours more than God's. – Anthony Burgess

৵৽

Few parts of my ministerial work have cost me more labor, or given me more pleasure, than catechizing. – S. Lavington

We must show our people, from first to last, that we are not merely saying good things in their presence, but directing what we say to them personally, as matters which concern them beyond expression. – Abp. Secker

❧

Many ministers are more chargeable with concealing truth, than affirming direct errors; with neglecting some part of their duty, than actually committing crimes; with not properly building the house, than willfully pulling it down. – Dr. Witherspoon

❧

May I be taught to remember, that all other studies are merely subservient to the great work of ministering holy things to immortal souls. – Henry Martyn

❧

How many ministers have been ruined by a love for company! – Lives

❧

Mr. Hinton was remarkable for taking early notice of religious impressions, especially in the minds of children. – Lives

Religion is not to be rendered abstract and curious. – Cecil

৯৯

It is indecent for him who is dedicated to the service of the church to give way to actions and discourse unsuitable to his character. – Bede's letter to Egbert, Abp. Of York

৯৯

Elegant dissertations upon virtue and vice, upon the evidences of revelation, or any other general subject, may entertain the prosperous and the gay; but they will not "mortify our members which are upon the earth;" they will not unstring calamity, nor feed the heart with an imperishable hope. – Dr. J. M. Mason

৯৯

Children should frequently be addressed in our ordinary discourses. Are we not verily guilty of despising the souls of these little ones, as if they were beneath us? – Dr. Bennett

৯৯

Ministers are apt to make too wide a distinction between seekers and believers. – Madan

We must study how to convince, and get within men, and how to bring each truth to the quick.
– Baxter

❧

Let us not forget that, should a season of remarkable prosperity be granted, it will probably prove an hour of fearful temptation to our souls. **– Bridges**

❧

For a want of personal religion, no abilities, natural or acquired, can compensate.
– J. Hinton's Life

❧

No man can be called eloquent, who speaks to an assembly on subjects, or in a strain, which none or few of them can comprehend. **– Blair**

❧

If there be any contest among the servants of the Lord, let this be the only one, -- who shall be most zealous in the service of his Divine Master; who shall be most earnest in prayer, most patient in hope, most lowly and gentle in spirit. **– Stewart's Thoughts, &c**

Truly I love to hear that preacher, who does not move me to applaud his eloquence, but to groan for my sins. – **Bernard**

꩜

The discourse of a preacher should go directly to the heart: it should be so framed as to prove and illustrate the subject, and work on the understanding and affections. – **Dr. Bates**

꩜

If you would be truly prosperous in your labors, aspire at once to possess a copious supply of the spirit of piety and of Jesus. – **A. Reed**

꩜

A good preacher fixes all our attention upon ourselves, a bad one draws it off, and diverts it from ourselves to other objects. – **Gisbert**

꩜

We shall find life in our doctrines, when there is doctrine in our life. – **Bridges**

In the ordinary course of event, the surest way to avoid reproach, and maintain the esteem of our people is, to act, on every occasion, faithfully and conscientiously. – Dr. MacGill

꙳

I will endeavor to be an example to the flock, going before them in the way to heaven. – M. Henry

꙳

Often have I heard sermons well arranged and well expressed, but one thing was wanting – the preacher did not put his heart into the sermon, and therefore did not put the sermon into my heart. – J. Cooke

꙳

Though studious, you may be idle; you may content yourself with thinking about doing good, and not do it. – Chrysostom

꙳

The life of a minister ought to shine with such a luster as to affect the heart, while it engaged the eye, and at once delight and instruct the minds of all who see it. – Chrysostom

Ministers should deal in truth, not dabble in theories. – Athenian

❧

Shall we feel mortified when immortal souls are saved, because we were not the instruments of their conversion? – J. A. James

❧

Why was the preaching of Baxter, Flavel, and Alleine, so happily successful in turning sinners from the errors of their ways, and in building up saints in faith and holiness? They plainly and earnestly "preached Christ crucified, the power of God, and the wisdom of God;" they directed the great truths of the gospel not only to the understanding, but to the heart. – Protest. Dissent. Mag. 1796

❧

Lukewarm pastors make careless Christians. – Fletcher

❧

Ought not this reflection always to accompany us? – Perhaps I am preaching my last sermon, or someone here is listening to his last warning. – D. Stoner

We are under strong temptation to cultivate the tree of knowledge, while we suffer the tree of life to pine away. – J. Campbell

సౌ≪

There is no habit so important as acquiring the power of fixing the thoughts. – Prac. Wisdom, &c

సౌ≪

There is something defective in a minister, unless his character produces an atmosphere around him, which is felt as soon as entered. – Jay

సౌ≪

I have no wish to be a popular preacher in any sense but one, namely, as a preacher to the hearts of the people. – L. Richmond

సౌ≪

A lazy minister in his younger years will make a poor old man. – Halyburton

By frequent pastoral visits, the minister should be continually moving among his people, diffusing instruction and reproof, exhortation and comfort. – Fletcher

⋙∘⋘

To prevail with our people to cultivate a spirit of prayer, is to obtain a mighty conquest.
– Brook

⋙∘⋘

The celebrated Dr. R. Bolton was designated "a gracious and soul-searching minister," and was greatly beloved by his people. When in years, and grey-headed, they used to point at him, and say, "when that snow shall dissolve, there will be a great flood;" and so it proved. Floods of tears were shed over his grave. – Brook

⋙∘⋘

We who preach that "the fashion of the world passeth away," should be dead to its vanities and pleasures. – Shanks

⋙∘⋘

Nothing is more to be avoided in the composition of a sermon than tame correctness.
– Leifchild

God will curse that man's labors, who is found in the world all the week, and then upon a Saturday goes to his study; whereas, God knows, that time were little enough to pray and weep in, and get the heart into a fit frame for the duties of the approaching Sabbath.
– Shepherd's Subjection to Christ

≫⋅≪

The way to enjoy the Divine presence, and be fitted for distinguishing service for God, is to live a life of great devotion and constant self-dedication to Him. – Brainerd

≫⋅≪

Holy Bradford studied on his knees: it is to be feared this example is oftener alluded to than followed. – Oliver Heywood

≫⋅≪

Some of the old divines were regularly in the habit of praying to God for direction in the choice of their texts. – Oliver Heywood

≫⋅≪

I value the office of a good minister more than the magnificence of an emperor.
– Oliver Heywood

Oh, what persuasion and entreating, what wooing and winning, what holy dexterity, what changing the speech to men's views and prejudices, is necessary to the proper discharge of this work! – R. Watson's Address to Lowe, &c

❧

I always feared sickness more than death, because sickness has made me unable to perform those offices for which I came into the world. – G. Herbert's letter to his mother

❧

Of President Edwards it is remarked, "His excellency as a preacher was very much the effect of his acquaintance with his own heart." – Lives

❧

If I had a thousand lives, I would think them all too little to employ in God's service. – Halyburton

❧

One of the failures in ministerial labor is owing to the neglect of detail and specification in the enforcement of moral topics. – Jay

What is considered to be the property of a good portrait, will not inaptly describe a good sermon – that it looks at all, though placed in different situations, as if it were glancing with a particular application to each, "I have a message from God unto thee." – Bridges

৵৹৻ও

They who teach not themselves are unfit to teach others. – Greenham

৵৹৻ও

I remember reading upon the pillar of a chapel, "This place will hold 1200 souls." How much are they worth? – Dr. Bennett

৵৹৻ও

If it were necessary to be chained to the gallies for seven years, in order to be admitted to so blessed a charge, who, that had a heart really affected, would hesitate to undergo the probation? – Kirke White

৵৹৻ও

Keep the end of your ministry continually in view, and I will engage that you will always preach practically. – Gisbert

I never grow cold, and dull, and pitiless to the souls of others, till I first grow too cold and careless of my own. – Baxter

᧬

The good preacher seeks the glory of Jesus Christ. The bad one uses the utmost strength of his eloquence to gain reputation. The latter handles trifles with elaborate language; the former elevates a plain discourse by the weight of his thoughts. – Julian Pomerius

᧬

I know it is my duty to study, and qualify myself in the best manner I can for public service: but this is my misery, I study and prepare that I may consume it upon my pride and self-confidence. – Brainerd

᧬

Your hearers may increase; your church may flourish, while your own devotional affections and virtuous dispositions greatly decline. – A. Booth

᧬

Were I more humble, I should go on more comfortably in my work. – Boston

It has been observed of Massillon, that at his death his memory was honored with the most eloquent of all funeral orations. – The Tears of The Poor!

ॐ∽ॐ

True eloquence is best known by its effects. Many an inflated address, which has cost the composer of it much thought and labor, is found destitute of every spark of moving oratory. – Select Mag. 1823

ॐ∽ॐ

What! Speak coldly for God, and for men's salvation: can we believe that our people must be converted or condemned, and yet can we speak in a drowsy tone? – Baxter

ॐ∽ॐ

Beware of curiosities and novelties in religion. – Halyburton

ॐ∽ॐ

Let every minister, while he is preaching, remember that God makes one of his hearers. – World

What in other professions is enthusiasm is, in ours, the dictate of sobriety and truth. – R. Hall

❧

If ministers love their people, they will forget their own dignity, that they may win some.
– **Perkins**

❧

The desire of appearing men of ability often prevents our being so.
– **Duke De La Roche-Foucault**

❧

If a preacher cannot so feel and think as to bend all subjects naturally and gracefully to Christ, he must seek his remedy in selecting such as are more evangelical. – **Cecil**

❧

Lord, grant that I may never rack a scripture simile beyond the true intent thereof; lest, instead of sucking milk, I squeeze blood out of it. – **Dr T. Fuller**

It is better to gain one soul to Christ, than to gain a world. – Oliver Heywood

৵৽

Never join in exposing weak brethren. – **Gurnall**

৵৽

That water is not the deepest that is thickest and muddy, nor that matter always the most profound when the preacher's expression is dark and obscure. – **Gurnall**

৵৽

Never choose a text you do not understand, nor put on any passage a fanciful or perverted meaning. – **Bradburn**

৵৽

Next to Christ, I have but one joy, the apple of the eye of my delights – to preach Christ my Lord. – **Rutherford**

Of many subjects it is proper for a minister to taste, on which he may not feed; for, if he would retain the freshness and power of his ministry, the science of salvation, the word of God, and the work of God, must be the study of his life. – R. Watson

༈

A preacher who is endued with a competent share of learning and fine parts, a retentive memory and good elocution, may recommend himself to the admiration of great numbers, while their consciences, in the hour of solemn reflection, bear testimony against him.
– A. Booth

༈

An intense desire for knowledge will not suffer a man to be idle. – Jay's Life of Winter

༈

A holy exemplary behavior gives a force and energy to sermons, which learning, genius, and eloquence, could never have procured them.
– Dr. Erskine

The Rev. John Newton used to say, his grand point in preaching was, "To break a hard heart, and to heal a broken heart." – Lives

❧

The judicious management of practical subjects is more difficult than the discussion of doctrinal points. – Eclectic, 1810

❧

It is always dangerous to prefer the indulgence of study to the active exercises of the ministry, or at least to "give ourselves wholly to reading," so as to neglect the work of pastoral instruction. – Bridges

❧

If a preacher desires to succeed, he should either be short, or at least seem so. – Gisbert

❧

Paul, that master workman, saith nothing of what he has wrought, but of what Christ has wrought by him. – M. Henry

Young divines, after the example of their elders, should be lovers of peace, and haters of contention. – Rob. Parker

❧

Count the whole world, in comparison with the cross of Christ, one grand impertinence. – Abp. Leighton

❧

How shall anyone be able to nourish others with the word, who does not first nourish himself therewith? – Quesnel

❧

You have been preaching half an hour, said Mr. R. to a brother clergyman, without one word directly aimed at the conscience. – Robinson's Life

❧

Tell Henry his poor father learnt his most valuable lessons for the ministry, and his most useful experience in religion, in the poor man's cottage. – L. Richmond

In a minister, a furious and choleric temper is of mischievous consequence. – Chrysostom

࿐

To seek to please men, will be to please their fancy rather than to gain their souls. – J. Crombie

࿐

Sermons gilt with words and not matter, are like images, that painted seem fair, but being looked into are found earth. – Wit's Commonwealth

࿐

Sylvester observes of Baxter, "When he spoke weighty soul-concerns, you might find his very spirit drenched therein." – Funeral Sermon for Baxter

࿐

That man knows but little of the dignity and importance of the priesthood, who can content himself with ordinary attainments. – Nelson's Life of Bp. Bull

The chief use of preaching consists in its direct and suitable application to the cases and consciences of our people. – Bridges

છે૰ઠ

The generality of our hearers are better judges of our examples than of our sermons. – Doddridge

છે૰ઠ

We are sufficiently honored, if, by any means, we may be instrumental in promoting that cause which employed the daily labors of God's incarnate Son, and at length cost him his very blood. – Doddridge

છે૰ઠ

It is a blessed sign when honors and exaltation tend to humble the mind of a minister. – Shanks

છે૰ઠ

Ministers who live and labor as they ought are generally well thought of. An exemplary piety, and a shining conversation, preserves the poorest of them from contempt. – Shanks

The great work of proclaiming salvation to a guilty world is the most honorable employment in the world. – Christian Guar. 1830

❧❧

Unprofitable eloquence is like cypress trees, which are great and tall, but bear no fruit. – Wit's Common-Wealth

❧❧

It is observed of the Rev. Wm. Strong, A.M., (1656), that "While he labored more to profit than to please, he never failed to please as well as profit, those who heard him."

❧❧

A pastor must sooner or later convert sinners, if he sincerely and earnestly calls them to repentance towards God, and faith in our Lord Jesus Christ. – Fletcher

❧❧

Let Jesus Christ be all in all. Study Christ, preach Christ, live Christ. – M. Henry

He points his eloquence against the vices, not the persons of mankind, and without chastising reclaims the wanderer. – Pliny

❧❧

A dull preacher makes a drowsy congregation. – Watts

❧❧

My first object is, to exhibit affection, earnestness, and a real desire that every sentiment and every sentence may profit the hearts of my hearers. – Leigh Richmond

❧❧

Preach no sermon without lifting up your heart to God both before and after its delivery, that it may be blessed to the people. – Henry Martyn

❧❧

Men frequently admire me, and I am pleased, but I abhor the pleasure. – Henry Martyn

Did the Spirit of truth more accompany the word of truth, how different would be the effects of preaching; and to obtain this blessed result, nothing else is wanting than that continual preaching should be accompanied by continual prayer. – **Douglas on prayer**

❧

Luther used to say, that he got more knowledge in a short time by prayer, at times, than by the study and labor of many hours.

❧

Forever bear in mind, that you ought not to be preachers only, you must be teachers of your flocks. – **Bp. Bagot to a young minister**

❧

A generalizing method of preaching, is speaking to everyone and to no one.
– J. Cooke

❧

That must be a worldly and criminal consideration, which makes us more anxious for our own glory, than for the glory of God.
– Massillon

One of the most important departments
of a Christian minister's labor is the care
and due culture of the rising generation.
– Con. Mag. 1822

⤟⤠

Wherever you are, remember you are a minister.
– Mrs. Judson to Dr. Wayland

⤟⤠

Preach frequently on the subject of missions.
I have remarked that when a minister
feels much engaged for the heathen, his
people generally partake of his spirit.
– Mrs. Judson to Dr. Wayland

⤟⤠

St. Paul preached with tears, Phil. iii. 18. A
hot iron, though blunt, will pierce sooner than
a cold one, though sharper. – Flavel

⤟⤠

The most effectual way of preaching Christ, is
to preach him in all his offices, and to declare
his law as well as his gospel, both to believers
and unbelievers. – John Wesley

The happiest fancy is not sufficient for
a Christian orator; we may admire the
exactness, the copiousness, and penetration
of his genius, but still we are to seek for the
spirit of Christianity, and the foundation of
our religion, both in him and his discourses.
– Gisbert

❧

In the first ages of Christianity, no man could
reasonably think of taking orders, unless he
had the spirit of martyrdom. – Burnett

❧

Which of us, alas! In looking back and
considering his opportunities of usefulness
and improvement, has no reason to deplore his
negligence? – Dr. MacGill

❧

Generals not explicated do but fill the people
with empty notions and their mouths with
perpetual unintelligible talk; but their hearts
remain empty, and themselves not edified.
– Bp. Taylor

Home scenes, as they are lovely or repulsive, form a beauteous halo round, or dark specks upon, the orb of your public character.
– J. A. James

છ−ન્ઉ

When a preacher wants purity, and becoming gravity, his character can never rise to that dignity of virtue which begets esteem and authority, which gives weight to his instructions and influence to his example.
– Rev. J. Owen, 1706

છ−ન્ઉ

The figures of the Christian orator should owe their beauty, force, and luster, more to the abundance of the heart, than the fineness of the understanding. **– Gisbert**

છ−ન્ઉ

Every minister in health should be up early in a morning. **– Paley**

છ−ન્ઉ

Many a preacher is now in misery who has a hundred times called upon his hearers to use their utmost care and diligence to avoid it.
– Baxter

One soul converted to God is better than thousands merely moralized, and still sleeping in their sins. – **Bridges**

❧❦

The celebrated Halyburton, in dying circumstances observed, "I loved to live preaching Christ, and I love to die preaching Christ."

❧❦

Speak in public as you do in private, when you speak in earnest, and from the heart. – **Blair**

❧❦

Mr. Gilpin remarks, that Mr. Fletcher's "preaching was perpetually preceded, accompanied, and succeeded by prayer."

❧❦

The great point in the management of your ministry is that you obtain the testimony of the great Shepherd when he shall appear.
– **Halyburton**

The unedifying converse of ministers is one great cause of the unsuccessfulness of the gospel. – **Boston**

⤳⤙

Some neglect strength of sentiment, and weight of matter, to force their empty words into a figurative style. – **Cicero**

⤳⤙

The consequences involved in saving a soul from death, and hiding a multitude of sins, will be duly appreciated in that world where the worth of souls, and the malignity of sin, are fully understood. – **R. Hall**

⤳⤙

For my own part, I would rather draw one single penitential tear from an obdurate sinner, than charm a court. – **Gisbert**

⤳⤙

If a man can only talk, and is destitute of the eternal Spirit, alas! What will it avail! – **Bradburn**

The prevalent attention to dress and outward appearance feeds the pride, and ruins more than half of our young ministers. – Mr. Thornton to Winter

৵৽

There is nothing so soothing, so exquisitely delightful, as study, when we feel we have God's blessing, and that we are laboring for his glory. – Kirke White

৵৽

Let the young minister preach on that subject which he feels at the present time most impressed on his own spirit. – Cooke

৵৽

When we would convince men of error by the strength of truth, let us withal pour the sweet balm of love upon their heads. – Cudworth

৵৽

The pleasure I have had but this week in preaching the gospel, I would not part with for a thousand worlds. – Whitfield

In the midst of great popularity, Dr. W. Gouge used to say, "I know more to abase me, than others do to exalt me." – Lives

જેન્જ

In the life of the Rev. Philip Skelton, it is said of him, that the most indulgent father could not have the welfare of his family nearer his heart, than he had that of his people.

જેન્જ

What do you preach for, but to benefit your people? And how can they be benefited unless they understand? – Dan. Taylor

જેન્જ

What! Shall the men of the world be more unwearied in seeking themselves, than the minister of the gospel in seeking the glory of his Master, Jesus, and the salvation of souls? God forbid! – Bostwick

જેન્જ

The ancients would have the goddess of persuasion to dwell always on the orator's lips, preside over his thoughts and words.

It is doubtful whether any preacher is worthy to appear in the pulpit, whose confidence in Divine truths is not strong enough to dispose him, if circumstances require, to seal those truths with his blood. – Fletcher

৵৽৹

Let doctrines be taught practically, and practice enforced by evangelical motives. **– W. Ome**

৵৽৹

It is observed of the Rev. Josh. Woodward, M.A. that "his presence in the streets, made the youths and the aged circumspect. It made the sober rejoice, and the guilty hid themselves in corners. – Palmer

৵৽৹

It was a saying with the Jews, that that was not true prayer in which the kingdom of God was not remembered.

৵৽৹

A true minister of Christ possesses his Master's grace, has received his Master's call, does his Master's work, bears his Master's yoke, aims at his Master's glory, and hereafter will receive his Master's reward.

More faith and more grace would make us better preachers. – Cecil

જ્જન

The minds of our divines should be joined together in peace and virtue, and should do and preach profitable things to the glory of God, and the utility of the church. – R. Parker

જ્જન

Mr. Winter, who was for a long time Mr. Whitfield's traveling companion, says of Mr. W., "I hardly ever knew him go through a sermon without weeping, more or less." – Jay's Life of Winter

જ્જન

If there be in the general conduct of the minister, more of the fine gentleman than of the primitive pastor, and more of the man of the world than of the "man of God," he deserves to be despised. – A. Booth

જ્જન

Paul was so taken with Christ, that nothing sweeter than Jesus could drop from his lips. – Charnock

How very seldom do we hear in the divisions of a discourse, any regard to the younger part of the audience!

కోపౌ

By listening to the habitual strain of some good men's preaching, we should be led to conclude, either that they had no unconverted hearers in their congregations, or that they had nothing to do with their conversion. – A. James

కోపౌ

Surely that applause is dearly bought which is gained at the expense of the blood of souls.
– J. Crombie

కోపౌ

To aim intensely and simply at one main object, to count every soul a kingdom, and to be more delighted to save a soul than to win a crown, this is the true spirit of the ministry. **– Bridges**

కోపౌ

Near the close of life, Andrew Fuller observed, "I wish I had prayed more for the assistance of the Holy Spirit, in studying and preaching my sermons."

Basil, a primitive bishop, was said to thunder in his preaching, and to lighten in his conversation.

છ∞લ

How odious is an idle preacher, who only does what he is obliged to do, and fears the censure of his brethren more than the displeasure of his Maker. – **Bradburn**

છ∞લ

If some preachers can but deliver a favorite sentiment of some great man, or some silvery expression, they fancy they have done something; but the words of God are the arrows that pierce. – **J. Cooke**

છ∞લ

Chrysostom used to say, that that scripture, "They watch for your souls, as those that must give account," filled his mind with constant awe.

છ∞લ

What have I affected? O thou Trier of the reins of men, what have I effected? Has one soul, but one soul, been lighted by this feeble ray towards the realms of peace and joy? If so, my God, I envy not the monarch's crown. – **Josh. Livingston**

Some think me happy because I have so few people and these not unruly: some think otherwise, because of the post and stipend: but none of these things move me, but that I am like to spend my strength in vain. – Boston

అీౖ

The Rev. C. Winter, when dying, could say, "I have sought the Divine glory more than my own interest." – Lives

అీౖ

The preacher who leaves it to his hearers to apply what he says to them, transfers to them the most essential part of his own business. – Gisbert

అీౖ

By a judicious direction of conversation, you may receive instruction from the meanest of your flock. – MacGill

అీౖ

Enticing words of man's wisdom debase your matter. Gold needs not to be painted. – M. Henry

He who preaches faithfully, will, in the end, never preach in vain. – Christian Observer

જાન્

Nothing can be more absurd, irrational, and contrary to the very design and end of speaking, than an obscure discourse – there is majesty in plainness. – South

જાન્

Those preachers have reason to tremble, who, though admired by the great, and caressed by the vain, are deserted by the poor, the sorrowful, and such as "walk humbly with God." – Dr. J. M. Mason

જાન્

My labors are acceptable, and not altogether unprofitable to my hearers: but what is this to me, if my own soul starve while others fed by me? – S. Pearce

જાન્

The Lord help men, and open their eyes before it be too late! For, either the gospel is not true, or there are few who, in a due manner, discharge that ministry which they take upon them. – Owen on Heb. VI. ii

I will be more careful and zealous to do good to souls by private instructions, exhortations, and reproofs. – **Rich. Mather**

ॐ

Oh! How did Paul sweeten all his sermons with love. – **T. Watson**

ॐ

What else do I desire, but that the turns and figures of the Christian orator should be the work of zeal, and of the Spirit of God; not of art, study, and affectation. – **Gisbert**

ॐ

True prophets, in the delivery of their messages, fear none but God, and dare say anything that God commands. – **Bp. Kerr**

ॐ

Nothing will give such power to our sermons, as when they are sermons of many prayers. – **Bridges**

One of the old divines used to say, that he was resolved his hearers should either quarrel with him, or with their sins.

❦

The more we converse with God and our own hearts, the fitter we shall be for the duties of our function. **– Bennet's Christian Oratory**

❦

The celebrated W. Perkins used to write in his books, "Though art a minister – mind they business."

❦

The word of God is too sacred a thing, and preaching too solemn a work, to be toyed and played with, as is the usage of some, who make a sermon nothing but matter of wit, and to flaunt it forth in a garish discourse. **– Gurnall**

❦

The corruptions of Christianity arise from the want of zeal, and from the indolence which pervades its teachers. **– Massillon**

Very excellent men excel in different ways: the most radiant stones may differ in color, when they do not in value. – **Howe**

৵৽

If we find that God blesseth our labors, this is the best seal of our ministry; as, if the arrow hit, it is a good sign that it was sent out of the bow. – **Fenner**

৵৽

P. Henry once wrote, on a studying day, "I forgot explicitly and expressly when I began to crave the blessing of God, and the chariot wheels drove accordingly. Lord, forgive my omission, and keep me in the way of duty!"

৵৽

I never desire a better proof of a faithless teacher than flattery. – **Bp. Hall**

৵৽

Scan your own hearts, and make use of the discoveries you get there, to enable you to dive into consciences, to awaken hypocrites, and to separate the precious from the vile. – **Halybutron**

*We should do more good if we were but
solicitous to do good.* – M. Henry

❧⤜

*How can I sustain the last judgment,
seeing so little fruit of my labors!*
– Gregory the First, 6th Century

❧⤜

*Mr. Shephard on his death bed (1649) observed
to a young minister three things: that the
studying every sermon cost him prayers, with
strong cries and tears; before he preached
any sermon, he got good from it himself; and
he always went up into the pulpit, as if he
were going to give up his accounts to his God.*
– Mather's History

❧⤜

*He is not the wisest minister who can plot most
for preferment, or preach best for applause:
no, no, but he that can most compose himself to
do good. "He that winneth souls is wise," Prov.
xi. 30.* – Fenner

❧⤜

*In the most faithful rebukes, in the most
solemn declarations of God's displeasure, a
preacher may give evidence of a disposition of
good-will and compassion.* – J. Newton

I sigh; I weep over opportunities which have been lost; opportunities to further the salvation of man, which to me may never, never more return. – Dr. Booker's farewell sermon

৵৽৽

No sermon can properly be complete, unless the preacher severally marks out, by the emphatic words "you" and "yours," the characters of his audience. – Picator, 1827

৵৽৽

Bunyan having preached with peculiar warmth and enlargement, some enraptured friends who had heard him, told him how sweet a sermon he had delivers. "Ay, (said the good man,) you need not remind me of that, the devil told me of it before I left the pulpit." – Toplady

৵৽৽

I think this is our business, to deal with the consciences of men in the plainest and most important things, such as are most apt to fasten upon and take hold of conscience.
– Howe

৵৽৽

I do not find that a sermon is good, if the preacher has not for his mark the building some corner of the walls of Jerusalem.
– Francis, of Sales

I will often humbly pray, that God would teach me to speak to children in such a manner, as may make early impressions of religion upon their hearts. – **Doddridge**

&

There must be a prudent mixture of severity and mildness both in your preaching and discipline. – **Baxter**

&

The conversion of one soul is better than the civilizing of a thousand. – **Fenner**

&

Something must be materially wrong when a man can be contented to live with a people in the sacred relation of a pastor, regardless whether his people thrive or pine away under him. – **C. Winter**

&

In answering the cases of conscience of the sick or afflicted, consider not who asks, but what is asked. – **Bp. Taylor**

*There is an ostentation of independence,
against which you must assiduously guard:
nothing can be more disgusting.* – Dr. MacGill

❧

*It is but too plain, that families of clergymen
are sometimes brought up to worldly
expectations, rather than as disciples of the
cross, and citizens of heaven.* – Bridges

❧

*Reflecting on the many years I have spent in
preaching the gospel, it was most bitter to me
to see how much time was gone, and how little
I had done for God.* – Boston's Memoirs

❧

*In the conclusion of his discourse, the preacher
should seize, warm, melt the heart, and should
dispose the hearer by persuasion, or compel
him by terror, to submit.* – Theo. St. John

❧

*It has been observed of Bp. Benson, that he
maintained his authority in the church by his
meekness.*

*I think we should speak oftener to children
about the love of Christ, and the joys of heaven.*
– David Jones

❧

*When we rub the consciences of men with our
sermons, presently their eye is at us, and if
they see us to be vain and worldly, this heals
them again: though the word wounded them,
yet this is an ease are as fair for heaven as he!*
– Fenner

❧

*Are you quite clear, that you are not negligent
in seeking the acquirement of some necessary
qualification for the more successful discharge
of your important and sacred duties?*

❧

*Melanchthon says of Luther, "I have often
found him in tears, praying for the church."*
– Funeral sermon 1546

❧

*Throw a devout, warm heart, into the
composition and delivery of every sermon.*

Weighty indeed is the office of a pastor. He must be an example to the flock, and yet must learn to keep himself humble. – Gregory

༶

Who can cause us to speak what we ought, and as we ought, but He in whose hands we and are words are? – Augustine

༶

The more I pray, the better I study. – D. Jones

༶

Of every preacher it out to be said, what is said of Perkins, the puritan, that he lived sermons; and as his preaching was a comment on his text, so his practice was a comment on his preaching. – Dr. T. Fuller

༶

A wicked bishop chiefly aims to gratify his passions, to confirm his authority, and to enrich himself. He avoids the laborious and humbling part of his office, and delights in the pleasant and honorable. A good one converts sinners to God by his preaching and example.
– Julian Pmerius, 5th Century

*There never was any revival of religion in
the church of God, any period of remarkable
prosperity in the labors of its ministers, but,
in all these instances, the preaching of Christ
Jesus the Lord, was the prominent, attractive,
commanding subject.* – Dr. Joseph Fletcher

࿐

*Oh, what a man ought a minister to be! How
holy and how wise a man!* – T. Walsh

࿐

*A good minister will carry the spirit of his
sermons into his ordinary conversation.*
– Hervey

࿐

*I never feel happy in the pulpit, unless
prepared for its duties by previous meditation
and prayer.* – D. Jones

࿐

*"Who can unlock the prison of despair?
Lead forth the captive to the light of day,
thaw the chilled energies, unwind the thread
perplexed, entangled? Who restores the pulse
of mental health, and bid the torpor cease,
the joyous current flow? O Prince of Life!
Thine is the power, and Thine the glory all!"*
– Lawson

"When I die, I shall then have my greatest grief and my greatest joy. My greatest grief, that I have done so little for Jesus; my greatest joy, that Jesus has done so much for me. My last words shall be, "Here goes an unprofitable servant." – Grimshaw

❧

"For our rejoicing is this, the testimony of our conscience, that in simplicity and godly sincerity, not with fleshly wisdom, but by the grace of God, we have our conversation in the world," – 2 Cor. i. 12

❧

A good man's sermons are lances to a bad man's conscience, and a balm to the penitent sinner. – Wit's Common-Wealth

❧

Every sermon should teach a sinner the way to God by Christ Jesus. – Wesley Mag. 1824

❧

Secret devotion must attend our public labors, if we would secure that Divine blessing, without which, neither the most eloquent preaching, nor the most engaging conduct, can command success. – Doddridge

Alas! If we do not sincerely practice all that we deliver, if our lives do not answer our teaching, we are like unto kine that give very good milk, but throw down the pail when they have done.
– Fenner

જ∼⸂

The reason why more success does not attend the preaching of the gospel is simply – success is not expected. – A. Fuller

જ∼⸂

I hope I know so much of the worth of souls, that I should think it a greater happiness to gain one soul to the Lord Jesus Christ, than to gain mountains of silver and gold to myself.
– M. Henry

જ∼⸂

If the orator is master of his art, some parts of his discourse will be so prudently composed, that there shall be no room for admiration.
– Cicero

જ∼⸂

The true learning of a gospel minister consists not in being able to talk Latin fluently, or dispute in philosophy, but in being able to speak a word in season to the wary soul.
– Philip Henry

In a sermon, everything should be expressed with regard to the audience, not to the preacher. – Gisbert

❧

Preachers without spiritual illumination, are like sun-dials in a cloudy day; they exhibit, by certain external marks, the design for which they are formed, but are of no use till the Sun of righteousness arise and shine upon them.
– E. Parsons

❧

There is a danger of making important statements of practical truth, without a direct and immediate reference to Christ. – Bridges

❧

Of all men in the world, we are in most danger of losing impressions of the reality of Divine things. – Shanks

❧

A minister shares in the good and in the evil of his parish: if they be good, it is to his praise; if they be evil, commonly he is guilty of it.
– Fenner

Such are the incalculable consequences of a
wife's character to a minister that, if she assist
him not in urging forward the machine, she
will hang as a dead weight upon the wheels.
– Cecil

⥣⥥

I lament that I have not been more diligent in
catechizing and exhorting the children of my
congregation. – Brown's Life

⥣⥥

A man never can arrive at the reputation of a
great preacher, while he appears such only to
the learned. – Gisbert

⥣⥥

If ministers have not the mind that was
in Christ Jesus, they will do little good.
– Dr. Fawcett

⥣⥥

Cursed are all preachers who aim at high,
hard, and neat things, and, neglecting the
saving health of the poor unlearned, seek their
own honor and praise, thereby to please one or
two ambitious people. – Luther's Table Talk

Eliot the missionary imposed a law upon himself, that he would leave something of God, and heaven, and religion, with all who should come near him. – Lives

৵৽

In visiting the sick, three things should steadily be kept in view, -- the influence of what may be said upon the person, if dying; the influence it may have on him, should he recover; and the influence it may have on persons in health about him.

৵৽

Secure to yourself time and opportunity on the morning of the sacred day, for the undistracted and undisturbed exercise of private meditation and prayer. – MacGill

৵৽

I hope I am at nothing but souls; and if I gain these, though I should lose all my worldly comforts by it, I shall reckon myself to have made a good bargain. – M. Henry

৵৽

The more I knew, the more humble I was. – Sir Matt. Hale

When ministers make the pulpit a scaffold, in which they descant upon their text, as thought the scriptures were a rattle for children and fools to sport with; or if they speak plain, yet skim the truth of the scriptures, and never dive deep to the edifying of the soul, a man may go to hell, though he do as they teach; people may hear them a thousand times, and no man made to cry out, "What have I done?" – **Fenner**

৵৽

The celebrated Robert Hall was once asked what he thought of a sermon that had created a sensation: Very fine, Sir," he replied, "but a man can't eat flowers.

৵৽

As much as possible, sermons ought to be carried on in a strain of direct address to the audience. – **Blair**

৵৽

Let me never fancy I have zeal till my heart overflows with love to every man living.
– **Henry Martyn**

৵৽

It is observed of Ascham, that he lost no time in the perusal of mean and unprofitable books.
– **Biog. Br.**

We do not sufficiently consider how much our personal religion is endangered from the very circumstance of religion being our profession.
– Bridges

&

It is said of Dr. Pocock, that "his whole conversation was one continued sermon, powerfully recommending the several duties of Christianity." **– Lives**

&

Let us remember, the end we aim at is not human, not carnal: our purpose is to saver souls. **– W. Perkins**

&

He, who conceives that simplicity of style and language has any natural connection with feebleness and vulgarity, shows himself totally unacquainted with the fundamental principles of taste. **– Gisborne**

&

I would rather fall with Christ, than reign with Caesar. **– Luther**

Hundreds of ministers have been ruined by indulging a thirst for the character of the great man, while they have neglected the far superior character of the good man. – A. Fuller

శ్రం

A minister should more especially be spiritual; our own phrases will rise up in judgment against us, if we be not spiritual. – Fenner

శ్రం

Ten thousand times blessed are they, who are honored of Christ to be faithful and painful in winning souls to Christ. – Rutherford's Letters

శ్రం

Souls are so precious, that we should not lose one for want of labor; but should follow them while there is any hope, and not give them up as desperate till there be no remedy. – Baxter

శ్రం

Though applause may be nectar to the ear, it is often poison to the soul. – Toplady

Insist much on the love of Christ.

❧

Clearness of pronunciation is to the ear, what clearness of perception is to the mind. – **Reybaz**

❧

How inexcusable are we, if we can preach the straitness of heaven's gate, and the narrowness of the way, and the strictness of the account the people shall be forced to give at the last day, and lay heavy burdens on other men's shoulders, and we ourselves not touch them with one of our fingers! Teach precisely, and live loosely; teach graciously, and walk broadly. This is gross hypocrisy; to act zeal and goodness in our private duties unto God. – **Fenner**

❧

Be not content with a sermon of mere doctrinal truths and articles of belief, but into every sermon bring something practical. – **Dr. Watts**

❧

What you hear and see in one family, report not in another. – **Dr. Gill**

Herein I perceive great need of watchfulness, and much care, lest my heart should put away that word from myself which I am pressing upon others. – Owen Stockton

✗✗

I should be happy, if always engaged for God. – Brainerd

✗✗

On the grand fundamentals of the gospel, an authoritative decision of statement becomes us, not allowing or supposing a doubt to belong to our message, any more than to our own existence. – Bridges

✗✗

Your hearers must feel the hand of the preacher probing their particular frailties. – Leifchild

✗✗

How careful should I, and all, be in the ministry, not to break the bruised reed! – Henry Martyn

Say nothing to gratify your own vanity.
– Gisbert

⤳⤶

We must preach Christ crucified in a crucified phrase. **– Fenner**

⤳⤶

It is better to serve the Lord in the gospel of his Son, than to serve the greatest prince on earth, in the highest station. **– Halyburton**

⤳⤶

Cornelius Winter once beautifully observed, in allusion to the words of our Savior, "That when he looked down upon the congregation, he saw everywhere his brother, his sister, his mother." **– Lives**

⤳⤶

A preacher hath three books to study – the bible, himself, and his people. **– Dr. R. Harris**

*Which is the best general method of preaching?
To convince, to invite, to offer Christ, to build
up. And to do this in some measure in every
sermon.* – John Wesley

వేజ

*He was not a library locked up, nor a book
clasped, but stood.* – Patrick's sermon for
Smith, 1652

వేజ

*The holy apostle, Paul, did not only bestow
a sermon upon his people, but was willing to
impart to them his very soul, if it might save
theirs.* – T. Watson

వేజ

*I can never do too much for Him who hath done
so much for me.* – Geo. Herbert

వేజ

*Did Augustine throw by his beloved Cicero,
because he could not find Christ there? And
shall we reckon that a burden, which Paul
counted a favor, to preach the unsearchable
riches of Christ?* – Hurrion

How can we bear the name of Christ, and bear to be called the ministers of Christ, and not mightily desire the conversion of souls? – Howe

꘎

Touching my ministry, I will be more painful and diligent in private preparation, by reading, meditation, and prayer. In and after preaching I will earnestly strive against pride and vainglory. Before and after preaching I will seek unto the Lord for his blessing upon his word, more carefully than in time past.
– Richard Mather

꘎

Oh! My brethren, if Christ be not preached, the doors of the sanctuary are opened in vain.
– Dr. Morison

꘎

Dr. Chadderton, who died 1640, used to say, "I desire as much to have my servants to know the Lord as myself." He was married fifty-three years, and during the whole of this period, never kept his servant from public worship to cook victuals. – Brook

In composing sermons, Dr. C. Mather used to pause at the end of every paragraph, and endeavor to make his own soul feel some holy impression of the truths it contained. – Lives

❦

In his sermons, he endeavored to infuse into the hearts of his hearer's right apprehensions, and warm thoughts, of the great things of the Christian religion. – Bp. Bedell's Life

❦

A man may as well expect to grow stronger by always eating, as wiser by always reading.
– Jer. Collier

❦

Many act, as if they thought this were all the work of a minister – to make a few sermons, read a few prayers, etc. No, no, a minister must be thoroughly furnished to every good work. – Morning Exercise, 1661

❦

Ministers are called angels. What care angels for fine houses, or great livings? They had rather be in the prison with Peter, than with Herod at the court. – Fenner

You may rise early, go to bed late, study hard, read much, and devour the marrow of the best authors; and, when you have done all, unless God give a blessing, be as lean and meager in regard of true and useful learning, as Pharaoh's lean kine were, after they had eaten the fat ones. – Bp. Sanderson

❧

In the houses where he sojourned, their hands fed one, but his lips fed many. **– Joseph Alleine's Life**

❧

You may possibly do more good by the sick bed, than in the pulpit. **– Bp. Hopkins**

❧

Life is too short to afford time even for serious trifles. Pursue what you know to be attainable; make truth your object, and your studies will make you a wise man. **– Cowper**

❧

One of the precepts which Epictetus gave to his disciples was, "Think with yourselves, on all occasions – I am a philosopher." O brethren, let us on all occasions recollect that we are ministers: the recollection will prove salutary. **– Grimshaw**

Use me, O Lord, I beseech Thee, as the
instrument of Thy glory: and honor me
so far, as either by doing or suffering Thy
appointments, I may bring praise to Thy
name, and benefit to the world in which I live.
– Grimshaw

೩∘ఆ

The office of the ministry, says Bp.
Grosseteste, (of the 13th century), requires
one, "whom no prejudice, passion, entreaty,
or gift, or partiality, can divert from the
path of rectitude, who delights in labor,
and whose whole desire is to profit souls."
– Hist. Of the Church

೩∘ఆ

"Holiness on the head; light and perfections on
the breast; harmonious bells below, raising the
dead, to lead them unto life and rest; -- thus
are true Aarons dressed. – **G. Herbert**

೩∘ఆ

Profaneness in my head: defects and darkness
in my breast; a noise of passions ringing me,
for dead, unto a place where is no rest, --Poor
priest! Thus am I dressed. – **G. Herbert**

Only another Head I have; another heart and breast; another music, making 'live, not dead! Without whom I could have no rest: -- In Him I am well dressed. – G. Herbert

꧁꧂

Christ is my only Head; my only heart and breast; my only music, striking me even dead, that to the old man I may rest, and be, in Him, new dressed. – G. Herbert

꧁꧂

So, holy in my head; perfect and light in my dear breast; my doctrine tuned by Christ, who is not dead, but lives in me, while I do rest: -- come, people; Aaron's dressed." – G. Herbert

SALUTARY COUNSELS

Reflect much on the indispensable and transcendent importance of personal religion.

❦

Aim, with the most conscientious solicitude, at purity of motive in all your ministerial engagements.

❦

Repress, to the utmost, the feelings of vanity and pride, and the undue desire of popular applause.

❦

Let the grand points in religion have the due prominence in your discourses.

❦

Aim, in preaching, at the utmost seriousness and earnestness of manner.

Let a deep sense of responsibility at the Divine tribunal secure ministerial fidelity.

❧

Let there be in your discourses the utmost clearness of discrimination between the two great classes of characters of which your hearers must necessarily consist.

❧

Let pointed appeals to the heart, and direct applications to the conscience, form a prominent feature in your discourses.

❧

Do not aim at a degree of originality to which you are not equal, or of which the subject under consideration does not admit.

❧

Study assiduously the best way of access to the human mind.

In your preparations for the pulpit, endeavor to derive from the subject on which you are about to preach, that spiritual benefit which you wish your hearers may derive.

࿇

Attach due importance to the devotional parts of public worship, and be solicitous to conduct them in a spirit of evangelical fervor.

࿇

Cherish earnest desires, and encouraging expectations of success.

࿇

Exercise a humble and entire dependence on the promised influences of the Holy Spirit.

࿇

Endeavor to adopt the most interesting and efficient methods of conveying religious instruction to the young.

Endeavor to regulate, on principles which an enlightened conscience will approve, the time devoted to pastoral visits and pastoral intercourse.

೭ঞ্ৰৄৢ

Cultivate, with daily solicitude, spirituality of mind.

೭ঞ্ৰৄৢ

Cultivate and display Christian zeal for the general interests of true religion, both at home and abroad.

೭ঞ্ৰৄৢ

Propose to yourself, as a model, the character of the apostle Paul.

೭ঞ্ৰৄৢ

Guard against every approach to a sectarian and party spirit; and cherish the feelings of Christian love to all who embrace the faith, and "adorn the doctrine" of the gospel.

Do full justice to the talents and excellences of other ministers, without the spirit of rivalry or jealousy.

వించ

Deem it not justifiable for a Christian pastor to indulge, beyond certain limits, in the pursuits of literature and science.

వించ

Suffer not the pressure of public engagements to contract, unduly, the exercise of private devotion.

వించ

Guard against levity of spirit and demeanor.

వించ

Cherish the strictest purity of thought, of sentiment, and of demeanor.

Cultivate and display the most delicate sense of honor in all the intercourses of life.

❧

Remember the pre-eminent importance of prudence and discretion.

❧

Study and display that courtesy, which is the essence of true politeness.

❧

Observe punctuality in all your engagements.

❧

Do not hastily abandon a station of usefulness, in which you have acquired a moral influence.
--Dr. H. F. Burden

FINAL THOUGHTS FROM
The First Book of Wit & Wisdom
by Basil Jackson

THINGS I SHOULD HAVE LEARNED
AS A CHILD

Affect vs. Effect

Affect as a verb means "to influence."
Example: Fear *affects* the mind.

Effect as a verb is "to bring about or cause."
Example: It is about time to *effect* some changes.

Affect as a noun refers to an individual's emotional state.
Example: The sad patient has a depressed *affect*.

Effect as a noun means "the result or the outcome."
Example: The effect of the change was gratifying.

❧

As a child, I learned a basic principle of hermeneutics:
"Wonderful things in the Bible I see;
Many of them put there by you and by me."

ॐ

God has not formulated a plan or blueprint
for your life; He has given you the ability to
make one directed to His glory.

ॐ

Opportunities are not bequeathed or
awarded, but usually result from hard work.

ॐ

It is impossible to understand the present in
isolation from the past.

There is a great difference between praying
and saying prayers.

༶

Human eloquence must never have
preeminence over the Word of God.

༶

God's truth will always be able to adapt to
and serve the immediate local needs and
outlook of each successive epoch, without in
any way being changed substantively.

༶

God expects me to do at least one loving act
each day.

The real art of a conversation is not only to say the right thing in the right place, but also to leave unsaid the wrong thing at the tempting moment.

൭ൟ

If you think there is good in everybody, you have not met everybody.

൭ൟ

When you become too wise to learn, you become too ignorant to teach.

൭ൟ

The essence of God's will for my life always involves the actualization of whatever potential or talent He has given.

ABOUT E. BASIL JACKSON

E. Basil Jackson, MD, JD, DLitt, is a Distinguished Professor of Psychiatry, Medicine and Law. Born in Ireland, and received his early education there. He studied at the Queen's University of Belfast Medical School and shortly after graduation received a fellowship in psychiatry at the Menninger School of Psychiatry in Topeka, Kansas.

After completion of training in Adult Psychiatry, he entered the Child Psychiatry program at the University of Rochester in Rochester, New York. Shortly after completing training as a pediatric psychiatrist, he became Director of Graduate Psychiatric Education at Marquette University School of Medicine in Milwaukee, Wisconsin. The American Board of Psychiatry and Neurology certified Dr. Jackson in Psychiatry, Child Psychiatry and

Forensic Psychiatry. Jackson also holds certification as a Psychoanalyst and in Addictionology and Compulsive Disorders. He has practiced these disciplines all of his professional life. He also holds doctorates in theology and law and is a member of the Bar of the State of Wisconsin. Presently Dr. Jackson continues to consult in the field of law and psychiatry, but his principal interest lies in the integration of faith and society.

APPENDIX

This index provides a brief bio of a partial list of the notable persons whose words appear in this collective work. It is an alphabetical listing.

SOME OF THE NOTABLE PERSONS QUOTED

Augustine -- Augustine of Hippo also known as Augustine, was Bishop of Hippo Regius (present-day Annaba, Algeria). He was a Latin philosopher and theologian from Roman Africa generally considered as one of the greatest Christian thinkers of all times. His writings were influential in the development of _ Christianity. Most scholars accept Augustine as the most important figure in the ancient Western church.

Bagot -- Lewis Bagot, D.C.L., (1783-1790) Bishop of Norwich.

Baxter -- Richard Baxter (1615-1691) was a spiritual and pastoral example to John Wesley. He was an English Puritan leader, poet, hymn-writer, and theologian. Baxter was known as "the chief of English Protestant Schoolmen."

Bridges -- George Wilson Bridges (1788–1863) was a writer, photographer and Anglican cleric. He was rector for the Jamaican parish of Manchester from 1817 to 1823. He then served the neighboring parish of St Ann from 1823 to 1837. He toured around the Mediterranean taking 1,700 early pictures including Egypt, Greece, the Holy Land and Mount Etna erupting. His last parish was in Gloucestershire.

Calvin – John Calvin (1509 –1564) was an influential French theologian and pastor during the Protestant Reformation. He was a principal figure in the development of the Christian theology later called Calvinism. After religious tensions provoked a violent uprising against Protestants in France, Calvin moved to Basel, Switzerland, where he published the first edition of his seminal work The Institutes of the Christian Religion in 1536.

Campbell -- The Reverend James Campbell (1705 - 1780) was a Scottish Presbyterian who came to America in 1730, but returned to Scotland at the end of his life.

Chrysostom -- John Chrysostom, Archbishop of Constantinople, was an important Early Church Father. Known for eloquence in preaching, public speaking, and his denunciation of abuse of authority by both ecclesiastical and political leaders. After his death, John was given the Greek epithet chrysostomos, meaning "golden mouthed" in English, and Anglicized to Chrysostom.

Edwards -- Jonathan Edwards (1703 –1758) was an American preacher and theologian. Edwards is known as America's most important and original philosophical theologian, and one of America's greatest intellectuals.

His theological work was broad in scope, but was often associated with Reformed theology, the philosophical study of being and knowing, theological determinism, and the Puritan heritage.

Felton-- Nicholas Felton (1556–1626) was an English academic, Bishop of Bristol from 1617 to 1619, and then Bishop of Ely. He was rector of St. Mary-le-Bow church in London, from 1597 to 1617; also rector at St. Antholin, Budge Row. He was Master at Pembroke Hall, Cambridge (1616-1619).

Fletcher -- John William Fletcher (1729-1785) was a contemporary of John Wesley and is often referred to as the "first theologian of Wesleyanism." Fletcher was renowned in the Britain of his day for his piety and generosity.

Gisbert --Blaise Gisbert (1657 – 1731) was a French Jesuit rhetorician and critic. He entered the Society of Jesus in 1672, and taught the humanities, rhetoric, and philosophy, after which he devoted himself for a long time to preaching. The pleasure that Gisbert took in discussing pulpit eloquence impelled him to write an essay on sacred eloquence (1702).

Hall -- Robert Hall (1764-1831) was an English Baptist Minister educated at King's College, Aberdeen. He preached for fifteen years in the Baptist church at Cambridge, and afterwards at Bristol.   Hall was an intellectual preacher of the highest order. His voice and pulpit manner were weak, but the order and sweep of his ideas held vast congregations spellbound.

Herbert – William Herbert (1778 –1848) was Dean of Manchester, and Rector of Spofforth, Yorkshire. He earned his doctorate from Merton College, Oxford. His knowledge in both ancient and modern languages and in his work he was both exact and extensive.

Hooker -- Thomas Hooker (1586-1647) was. born in Leicestershire, England. After his religious conversion, he rose into the leadership of the Puritan movement in England due to his keenly reasoned reflections upon Christian life and the meanings of Biblical passages. He became the founder of the Colony of Connecticut.

Jewel – Bishop John Jewell (1522-1572), Bishop of Salisbury and Anglican Reformer. Jewell's works are an excellent statement of Protestant, Reformed, and Anglican Churchmanship.

Perkins – William Perkins (1558 – 1602) was a clergyman and Cambridge theologian who was one of the foremost leaders of the Puritan movement in the Church of England. In 1585, he became rector of St. Andrew's Church in Cambridge, a post he would hold until his death.

London Lives (1690-1800) a project dealing with crime, poverty, and social policy. It is a fully searchable edition of 240,000 manuscripts from eight archives and fifteen datasets, giving access to 3.35 million names.

Leighton — Robert Leightgon, Archbishop of Glasgow (1611-1684).

Livingston -- David Livingstone (1813 –1873) a
Scottish Congregationalist pioneer medical missionary
and an explorer in Africa. His meeting with H. M. Stanley
gave rise to the popular quotation, "Dr. Livingstone, I
presume?"

Newton -- John Newton (1725 –1807) a man who
moved from disgrace to Amazing Grace. John wrote his
own epitaph: "John Newton, Clerk, once an infidel and
libertine, a servant of slaves in Africa, was by the rich
mercy of our Lord and Saviour, Jesus Christ, preserved,
pardoned and appointed to preach the Faith he had long
laboured to destroy".

Reynolds -- Sir Joshua Reynolds (1723 –1792)
was the most important and influential of 18th century
English painter.

Secker – Thomas Secker (1693-1768) Archbishop of
Canterbury.

Wesley -- John Wesley (1703 –1791) was an Anglican
cleric and Christian theologian. Wesley is largely credited,
along with his brother Charles Wesley, as founding the
Methodist movement. Methodism was a highly successful
evangelical movement in the United Kingdom, which
encouraged people to experience Jesus Christ personally.
Wesley's teachings, known as Wesleyanism, provided the
seeds for the modern Methodist movement, the Holiness
movement, Pentecostalism, the Charismatic Movement,
and Neo-charismatic churches, which encompass
numerous denominations across the world.

www.ingramcontent.com/pod-product-compliance
Lightning Source LLC
Chambersburg PA
CBHW021332090426

42742CB00008B/583